THE
HOUSEPLANT
LIBRARY

PLANTS FOR
WARM
ROOMS

Kenneth A. Beckett

Salem House

First published in the United States by
Salem House Publishers, 1989, 462 Boston Street,
Topsfield, Massachusetts, 01983.

Conceived and produced by
Swallow Books, 260 Pentonville Road,
London N1 9JY

ISBN: 0 88162 385 7
Art Director: Elaine Partington
Editor: Catherine Tilley
Designers: Jean Hoyes and Hilary Krag
Studio: Del & Co
Typesetters: Bournetype, Bournemouth
Printed in Italy by Imago Publishing Limited

Author's acknowledgments
The great majority of pictures in this book are of plants
growing in botanical and private gardens. My wife Gillian,
who took most of the colour transparencies, and I are
particularly grateful to the following people for their
cooperation in allowing us access to their plant
collections behind the scenes: Mr C. D. Brickell, formerly
Director of the RHS Gardens, Wisley, Dr R. D. Shaw,
Curator of the Royal Botanic Garden, Edinburgh and
Mr J. B. E. Simmons, Curator of the Royal Botanic
Gardens, Kew. We are especially indebted to
Mr L. Maurice Mason for allowing us unlimited time
among his treasures at Talbot Manor, Fincham, Norfolk
over the years. As a result, more of his plants feature in
this book than anyone else's.

INTRODUCTION

Central heating not only provides a comfortable environment for man, but also for some of the tropical plants with which he evolved. It enables most homes to maintain the recommended minimum room temperature for the majority of plants, which by day is about 20°C (68°F), and by night is 13°C (55°F). This temperature range enables us to grow a wide variety of tropical and sub-tropical plants.

Although our houseplants come from a wide range of the world's climates, by far the greater number come from the tropics and sub-tropics, mainly from forests, jungles and deserts. During the past 30–40 years, these warm regions have been ransacked for plants adaptable enough to thrive in the home. All the plants described in this book will grow indoors, though some would thrive more satisfactorily in a conservatory or greenhouse. The really successful species are those that come from drier climates, for instance, most cacti and other succulents, and the genera *Streptocarpus* and *Saintpaulia*. Most of the tropical bromeliads are also excellent houseplants. They are largely epiphytic, that is, they exist on another plant, such as a tree, and are therefore subject to a widely fluctuating range of temperatures, exposure and degree of wetness and dryness. There are also a surprising number of tropical orchids which can be successfully grown in a warm room.

Siting, choosing and buying

Warmth is not the only factor when choosing a plant for this environment. If you intend to place it on a wall away from a window, make sure it likes shade. Similarly, if you position it on a window sill, check that it will thrive in direct sunlight. Basic information on the light and water requirements of all the plants described here are given in easily understood symbols at the beginning of each entry.

Although the quality of houseplants, whether bought from a nursery, garden centre or multiple store, is generally good, it still pays to shop around for the best specimens. Do not buy plants that look pale and weak, or have limp, flecked or crippled leaves. If the plant has flowers or buds, watch that they do not shed readily when the plant is gently shaken. In winter time get a new plant home as soon as possible. Prolonged chilling can result in partial or total loss of leaves, or withering of leaves and flower buds.

Watering

Giving too much or too little water to a plant in a pot is the main cause of root failure and death. For the beginner, knowing when to water can be a serious problem. In general, aim to keep the soil moist, but not wet. Too much water will result in a sour, sodden soil that is ideal for root rot diseases. Too little water can produce a slow-growing plant with small leaves and flowers which are very prone to wilt or to being prematurely shed. The easiest way to decide when a plant needs water is to test the soil surface with your finger tip. If when you scratch down to about 1cm (½in) the soil feels dry or barely damp, give it a thorough watering. This means using enough water to fill up the gap between the soil surface and the pot rim. If the plant is a cactus or succulent let the soil be almost totally dry between waterings, and give it little or no water from mid-autumn to mid-spring. Treat orchids in the same way, but keep watering them throughout winter.

Humidity

Many of the plants described in this book come from areas of high rainfall, where the air is humid, at least during the growing season. Although many of these are remarkably tolerant of the dry air in most homes, they will be much healthier in more moist air, especially the ferns and orchids. Even cacti and succulents need humidity when they are growing. To increase the humidity, try plunging the pots into deep trays of moist peat. Alternatively, stand the pots on shallow trays of flooded gravel, making sure the water surface is just below the top of the stones. A third method is to use a fine droplet (mist) sprayer to wet the leaves at least once a day (except when temperatures drop below the average minimum).

Feeding

Sooner or later, the nutrients in a plant's potting soil will be exhausted and growth will slow to a standstill, the lower leaves will fall and all the new leaves will be much smaller than usual, and often pale or tinged with red or purple. Before this extreme state of starvation is reached, you should begin feeding the plant. This can be done easily by applying one of the formulated liquid feeds available from garden centres, mixed according to manufacturer's instructions. For a quick tonic, the so-called foliar feeds are very useful. These contain highly soluble fertilizers as well as a wetting agent, and should be mixed with water and sprayed on to the foliage.

Top-dressing

Those plants which are kept in a pot for a long time should be top-dressed annually in spring. Use a small hand fork or large kitchen fork to strip away the top layer of soil and fine roots, and remove about a sixth to a quarter of the total depth of the root ball. Do not damage the larger roots. Replace the discarded layer with fresh soil that contains one of the granular, slow-release general fertilizers. Finally, firm the soil around the plant and water it well.

Pruning

Perennials, shrubs and climbers have a tendency to grow too large, and will need cutting back from time to time. Climbers and shrubs are best thinned out to let in light and air when dormant or after flowering. Cut out whole stems or branches to their bases or to ground level; the remaining growth can be shortened by a quarter to a third. Evergreen perennials such as *Strobilanthes*, *Ruellia*, *Hemigraphis* and *Hypoestes* can be dealt with in the same way, but the remaining stems should be cut back by at least a half. Deciduous or semi-deciduous perennials, for instance, *Sinningia* and *Smithiantha*, should be cut back to ground level as the leaves yellow.

How to use this book

This book contains a selection of the most suitable and readily available plants for warm rooms, together with descriptions of the plants in their mature state, and their requirements (temperature, watering, and so on). These are given in the symbols, which are explained below. From this, you should be able to select a plant which meets your requirements exactly, and which will thrive in your home or conservatory. Although, as far as possible, technical terms have not been used in the main text of the book, there have been occasions when it has been impossible to avoid them. They are all explained in full in the glossary on page 63.

Symbol key

Cultural requirements and overall plant shape/growth habit are summarized in the form of at-a-glance symbols beside each entry. These provide quick reference and supplement the main description of the plant.

Light requirements

☀ Full sun

☀ Partial shade

● Full shade

Watering requirements

Light – Allow rooting medium to dry out completely between waterings.

Medium – Allow surface of rooting medium to dry out between waterings.

Heavy – Keep entire rooting medium moist at all times.

Plant habit/shape

☥ Erect

⇌ Spreading/prostrate

— Mat-forming

♀ Bushy

⋔ Weeping

⚶ Climbing/Scrambling

⌣ Rosette-forming

⋔ Pendent/Trailing

⫿ Tufted/Fan-like/ Clump-forming

Ω Globular (or cylindrical)

AESCHYNANTHUS
Gesneriaceae

Origin: *India, China and Malaysia. A genus of 80 species of evergreen trailing and climbing sub-shrubs, many of which grow epiphytically, that is, perched on another plant; they make splendid, colourful indoor plants. The lance-shaped to oval leaves are often rather fleshy and are carried in pairs. The showy, tubular, and sometimes hooded flowers are red or orange and form clusters at the ends of the stems. They are followed by berry-like fruits which are often white in colour. The trailing species are most effective when grown in hanging baskets, but those which climb are best grown in a pot or pan supported by a moss stick. Propagate by cuttings in spring or summer.* Aeschynanthus *derives from the Greek* aischune, *shame and* anthos, *a flower, suggesting rather oddly that the flowers blush for shame!*

Below *Aeschynanthus radicans*
Bottom *Aeschynanthus tricolor*
(in bud)
Bottom right *Aeschynanthus*
speciosus

Species cultivated

A. lobbianus Lipstick vine
An epiphyte, trailing or climbing weakly to 60cm (2ft) in height. The leaves are elliptic. Flowers grow to 4cm (1½in) long, are crimson with a yellow throat and a silky, dusky-red calyx. A good hanging basket plant, flowering in spring and summer. Considered by some to be a form of *A. radicans.*

A. radicans Java, Malaysia
An epiphytic plant with trailing or weakly climbing stems, compact in habit. Leaves are elliptic to oval, about 4.5cm (1¾in) long. Flowers grow to 5cm (2in) long, red with a green calyx streaked with purple-red. Botanists now consider that *A. lobbianus* is a form of this very variable species.

A. speciosus (*A. splendens, Trichosporum splendens*) Java, Borneo, Malaysia
This trailing plant grows to 60cm (2ft). Leaves are often borne in

whorls, pale green, waxy in texture and 7–10cm (2¾–4in) long. Flowers are 5–8cm (2–3in) long, bright orange, marked in the throat with red-brown, opening from summer to autumn.

A. tricolor Malaysia

A trailing plant, growing to about 30cm (1ft) long. Leaves are 2.5cm (1in) long, oval and lobed to make a heart shape, dark green above, paler beneath. Flowers grow to 4cm (1½in) long, are red with black and yellow stripes on the upper lobes and emerging from a dark bowl-shaped calyx, usually in pairs from the upper leaf axils.

ANANAS

Bromeliaceae
Pineapples

Origin: *Tropics of Central and South America. A genus of five perennial evergreen species. In the wild, unlike most bromeliads, these plants grow on the ground rather than being epiphytic (growing perched on another plant). They are clump-forming with erect rosettes of sword-shaped, spiny-edged leaves. Three-petalled, red or blue flowers are borne in spikes and are followed by fleshy fruits which fuse to form a syncarp – the familiar pineapple. The species described are*

Ananas bracteatus 'Striatus'

well-tried and durable pot plants. Propagate by suckers or by the leafy shoots which cap the fruits (slice off and plant in a propagating frame at 21–26°C [70–80°F]). Ananas *is the South American (Tupi) name for these plants.*

Species cultivated

A. bracteatus Wild/Red pineapple Brazil, Paraguay
Leaves are dark green, growing to 1.2m (4ft) in the wild (less in pots), with well-spaced spines around the leaf edges. Flowers are lavender with pink-red bracts on the flowering stems and beneath the blossoms. Fruits are brownish-red. *A.b.* 'Striatus' ('Tricolor') has leaves edged with yellow and a bronze-green centre with red spines.
A. comosus (*A. sativus*) Pineapple Brazil
Shorter, channelled leaves grow to 90cm (3ft) (less in pots), grey-green with small, closely set spines around the leaf edges. Flowers are purple-blue with green bracts. Improved forms are commercially grown for their fruits, and variegated forms for ornament. *A.c.* 'Porteanus' is olive-green with a central yellow stripe. *A.c.* 'Variegatus' (Ivory pineapple) has leaves with broad, cream edges.

APHELANDRA

Acanthaceae

Origin: *Tropical and sub-tropical America. A genus of 20 species of evergreen shrubs including several well-tried houseplants. They have opposite pairs of elliptic to oval, leathery leaves, often veined or mottled grey-silver or white, and dense spikes of tubular, two-lipped flowers at the ends of the stems, sometimes with coloured bracts. Propagate by cuttings of young shoots in spring or summer, or by seed in spring.* Aphelandra *derives from the Greek* apheles, *simple and* aner, *male, the anthers having one cell only.*

Aphelandra squarrosa

Species cultivated

A. squarrosa Zebra plant Brazil

Grows to 1.2m (4ft) or more. Leaves are 15–25cm (6–10in) long, oval, deep glossy green with contrasting white veins. Flowers and bracts are bright yellow, the latter sometimes having red edges, opening from late summer to winter. *A.s.* 'Louisae' is more compact with smaller leaves and makes a good pot plant. Several cultivars are available, varying in vigour, flower shade and patterning.

BEGONIA
Begoniaceae

Origin: *Widely distributed in tropical to warm temperate climates, most frequent in South America, but almost absent from Australasia and the Pacific Islands. A genus of 900 mainly perennial species, including some sub-shrubs and climbers. Although very variable, most have characteristic lopsided, ear-shaped leaves often with beautiful markings. Flowers are dioecious, that is, with single-sexed flowers on individual plants, and usually grow in clusters, with four to five (rarely two) tepals, the ovaries being winged or strongly angled. Some species are tufted and sub-shrubby with a fibrous root system, others are rhizomatous or tuberous. Propagate rhizomatous and tuberous species by division, or by leaf or stem cuttings, or by seed. Most species and hybrids in this huge genus make very good houseplants.* Begonia *was named for Michel Bégon (1638–1710), patron of botany and at one time Governor of French Canada.*

Species cultivated

B. × 'Cleopatra'

A handsome pot plant of hybrid origin. Leaves are maple-like, deeply lobed and toothed. They are yellow-green strongly suffused with pinkish-brown.

Below left Begonia × 'Cleopatra' *Below* Begonia masoniana

B. masoniana Iron cross begonia S.E. Asia

Rhizomatous; low-growing to 15–20cm (6–8in) or more. Leaves are very distinctive, being broadly oval to 20cm (8in) or more long with a strongly puckered surface, yellow-green with a bold, dark reddish-brown pattern very like the German Iron Cross. Flowers are small, greenish-white and insignificant and therefore this plant is usually grown for its leaves.

CALADIUM

Araceae

Origin: *Tropical America and West Indies. A genus of 15 species of perennials. They have underground tubers from which arise beautiful long-stalked, heart- to lance-shaped leaves. The flowers are in small, arum-like spathes but are fairly insignificant. This plant has extremely colourful leaves and is excellent for the home away from direct sun. Dry off and keep dormant for the winter. Propagate by offsets or division of tubers.* Caladium *is derived from the Malayan common name* kaladi, *misused for this genus.*

Species cultivated

C. × hortulanum Angel's wings

The name for the many hybrid cultivars derived from *C. bicolor* and *C. picturatum.* Leaves are triangular to heart-shaped, ranging in colour from white to pinks and reds with variable amounts of green. Those with white and pink leaves are more liable to sun scorch and damage than the darker-coloured ones, which tend to have firmer leaves. Many named cultivars are grown.

Caladium × hortulanum
'Fire Chief'

Above *Calathea picturata*
Left *Calathea makoyana*

CALATHEA

Marantaceae
Peacock plants

Origin: *Tropical America and West Indies. A genus of 150 species of evergreen perennials of tufted or clump-forming habit, some with tubers. The small, asymmetrical flowers are rarely produced on small pot-grown plants. They are grown for their attractively patterned, oval to lance-shaped leaves and make excellent house and conservatory plants. Propagate by division at potting time.* Calathea *derives from the Greek* kalathos, *a basket, from the flower clusters which supposedly resemble a basket of flowers as they sit within their bracts.*

Species cultivated
C. makoyana (*Maranta makoyana*) Peacock plant Brazil
Leaf stalks grow to 15cm (6in) or more, blades are broadly oval to 20cm (8in) or more, yellow-green above, patterned with fine lines and alternate large and small ovals in dark green, giving a supposed likeness to a peacock's tail. The undersurface of the leaf has the same patterning in purple.
C. picturata Brazil, Colombia, Venezuela
Leaf stalks grow to 20cm (8in), blades to 15cm (6in) or more, elliptic,

deep olive-green above marked with silvery lines along the midrib and parallel to the leaf edges. *C.p.* 'Argentea' has silvery-surfaced leaves with a dark green edge. In *C.p.* 'Vandenheckei' the silvery central line is feathery and the outer lines jagged.

CAMPELIA
Commelinaceae

Campelia zanonia
'Mexican Flag'

Origin: *Mexico to Brazil and West Indies. A genus of one evergreen perennial allied to* Dichorisandra, Geogenanthus *and* Tradescantia. *The variegated cultivar makes a striking specimen plant. Propagate by cuttings in summer. The derivation of* Campelia *is unknown.*

Species cultivated
C. zanonia
Tending to form erect clumps, the sturdy, sparingly branched stems reach 60–120cm (2–4ft) in height. Leaves are broadly lance-shaped to elliptic, 18–30cm (7–12in) long, rich green and rather lustrous.

CHAMAEDOREA
Palmae

Chamaedorea elegans

Origin: *Mexico to northern South America. A genus of 100 species of small palms, many of which send out suckers, with bamboo-like stems and pinnate, sometimes smooth-edged, leaves. The flowers are dioecious (of single sex on individual stems) in hanging or erect, spike-like inflorescences followed by single-seeded berry-like fruits. They are very successful pot or tub plants and can be grown in the conservatory or home provided the atmosphere is not too dry. Propagate by seed in spring, which germinates readily if kept at 20–24°C (68–75°F), or by division of those with suckering stems.* Chamaedorea *derives from the Greek* chamai, *dwarf and* dorea, *a gift, the bright fruits of some species being easily reached when ripe.*

Species cultivated
C. elegans (*Neanthe elegans*) Parlour palm, Dwarf mountain palm
Mexico, Guatemala
This plant has slender stems reaching 3m (10ft) that send out suckers. Leaves are 60–120cm (2–4ft) long, pinnate, with broadly lance-shaped leaflets, dark green and leathery in texture.
C.e. 'Bella' (*Neanthe bella*)
It is similar to *C. elegans*, but with a maximum height of about 1m (3ft) and slower growing. A very tolerant palm for the home which will flower in a pot, producing erect clusters of pale yellow flowers followed by small, globular fruits.

CODIAEUM
Euphorbiaceae

Origin: *Malaysia to the Pacific Islands and northern Australia. A genus of 15 species of evergreen shrubs of which only one is cultivated. It makes an excellent house or conservatory plant. Propagate by tip cuttings in spring or summer.* Codiaeum *derives from the Indonesian (Moluccan) common name* kodiho.

Codiaeum variegatum pictum

Species cultivated

C. variegatum pictum Croton, Joseph's coat Malaysia, Polynesia, not known truly wild

A shrub growing to 1m (3ft) or more. Leaves are leathery, glossy, basically oval but in the many cultivars available varying from narrow and straight to oak- or fiddle-shaped, sometimes waved and twisted. Their colour is basically green, then spotted, blotched or suffused with shades of yellow, orange, red and pink, the colouring usually strongest along the veins. Flowers are small and borne in axillary racemes on larger plants.

COLEUS
Labiatae

Origin: *Tropical Africa and Asia. A genus of 150 species of perennials, annuals and sub-shrubs. They have opposite pairs of oval, stalked leaves, and small, tubular, two-lipped flowers which are borne in whorls on a spike-like inflorescence. Usually grown as annuals, they are colourful plants for the home and conservatory. Extra large plants can be obtained by potting on into larger containers each spring. Propagate by seed in spring, or by cuttings in spring and late summer.* Coleus *derives from the Greek* koleos, *a sheath, the stamen filaments being united to enclose the style.*

Coleus blumei

Species cultivated

C. blumei Flame nettle, Painted nettle Java

A shrub growing to 60cm (2ft), sometimes more. Leaves are oval to heart-shaped, toothed, often hairy beneath. Flowers are small, white or blue, borne in a spike-like cluster.

COLUMNEA

Gesneriaceae

Origin: *Tropical America. A genus of 200 species of evergreen perennials and sub-shrubs, the majority of which are epiphytic. They have opposite pairs of rounded to very narrow leaves which, in many species, are turned so that all face in the same direction. Stems are climbing or trailing and the showy flowers are borne singly or in small groups in the leaf axils, each flower being tubular with a prominently four-lobed mouth, the upper lobe often longer and forming a hood. They make fine pot plants, the trailing species being particularly decorative in a hanging basket. Propagate by cuttings from non-flowering stem tips in spring or summer, or by seed in spring. Columnea was named for Fabio Colonna (1567–1640) using the Latin form of his name, Fabius Columna, an Italian botanist and author of the first work to use copperplate illustrations.*

Columnea 'Stavanger'

Species cultivated

C. gloriosa Goldfish plant Costa Rica

Stem hangs to a length of 1m (3ft) or more. Leaves are oval to oblong, growing to 3cm (1¼in), and covered with short brown hairs. Flowers are 8cm (3in) long, and very showy, being fiery-red with a yellow throat. They are freely produced from late autumn through the winter to early spring. It makes a fine plant for a hanging basket. *C.g.* 'Superba' ('Purpurea', 'Rubra', 'Splendens') has the leaves densely covered with purple hairs.

C. microphylla Goldfish plant Costa Rica

Leaves broadly oval to almost rounded, growing to 1cm (⅜in) long, brown-hairy. Flowers are 6–8cm (2½–3in) long, very free-flowering. An excellent plant for a hanging basket.

Hybrid cultivar

'Stavanger' (*C. microphylla* × *C. vedrariensis*) Norse fire plant, stems are trailing and well branched, growing to 60cm (2ft) long, with small, rounded, rather lustrous leaves. Flowers are 8cm (3in) long or more, cardinal-red with a prominent helmet-shaped upper lip.

Columnea microphylla (and *Selaginella kraussiana*)

CORDYLINE

Agavaceae (Liliaceae)

Origin: *Tropical and warm temperate areas of Australasia and Malaysia with one species in South America. A genus of 15 species of evergreen trees and shrubs often confused in cultivation with Dracaena, q.v. They have erect, often solitary stems, each one ending in a palm-like tuft of long, sword-shaped leaves. The flowers are small, but carried in large panicles at the ends of the stems, followed by coloured berries. Cordylines make attractive plants for the conservatory or home. Propagate by seed in spring or by suckers detached in late spring, or by 6cm (2½in) long stem sections in early summer, treating both these as cuttings until well rooted. Cordyline derives from cordyle, a club, probably alluding to the swollen stem bases of some species which give a rather club-like appearance.*

Cordyline terminalis

Species cultivated

C. terminalis (*Dracaena terminalis*) Ti tree Tropical Asia, Polynesia

Stems are erect, 1–4m (3–13ft) tall. Leaves are broadly lance-shaped, 30–60cm (1–2ft) long and up to 15cm (6in) wide, carried on distinct stalks 5–15cm (2–6in) long. Flowers are about 6mm (¼in) long, white, sometimes reddish or purplish. The red fruits grow to 8mm (⅓in) wide. A number of leaf colours are available: *C.t.* 'Baptistii' has deep green to bronze leaves striped with creamy-yellow and pink; *C.t.* 'Tricolor' has broader leaves striped with cream, pink and red.

Cryptanthus acaulis

CRYPTANTHUS
Bromeliaceae
Earth stars

Origin: *Brazil. A genus of 22 species of evergreen perennials which form rosettes and in the wild live largely on the ground, unlike many other bromeliads. They have narrow, evergreen, leathery leaves, usually with toothed edges, and are patterned or coloured. The flowers are small, five-lobed, usually white, and borne in spikes. They are good plants for the conservatory or home, often being used in dish gardens. Propagate by removing suckers or offsets and treating them as for cuttings. Cryptanthus derives from the Greek* krypto, *to hide and* anthos, *a flower, the flower buds being concealed by bracts.*

Species cultivated
C. acaulis Green earth star
This plant has flattened rosettes 15–30cm (6–12in) wide. Leaves are lance-shaped to narrowly triangular, wavy- and spiny-edged, green covered with white scales. *C.a.* 'Ruber' has smaller leaves with purplish-bronze on the edges and centres of the leaves, and fawn-coloured scales.

DICHORISANDRA
Commelinaceae

Origin: *Tropical America. A genus of about 35 species of perennials, those described below having handsome lance-shaped foliage and clusters of attractive flowers at the ends of the stems. They look effective when planted out in a conservatory border and can be grown in containers in the home. Propagate in early spring by*

division, or by cuttings in summer. Dichorisandra *derives from the Greek* dis, *twice,* chorizo, *to part and* aner, *male, referring to the way in which two of the six stamens spread apart from the others.*

Species cultivated

D. reginae (*Tradescantia reginae*) Peru
Stems are more or less erect, branching occasionally and slowly forming clumps, eventually up to 60cm (2ft) or more in height. Leaves are in two ranks, lance-shaped to elliptic, growing up to 18cm (7in) long, red-purple below, dark purplish, glossy green above with two silvery bands and lesser streaks which tend to fade with age. Flowers are about 2.5cm (1in) wide; each of the three blue-purple petals has a white base; they are produced in compact panicles in summer, but only on long-established plants and even then not profusely – however, this plant is really grown for its attractive leaves and any flowers are a bonus.

Dichorisandra reginae

DIEFFENBACHIA

Araceae
Dumb canes

Origin: *Tropical America and West Indies. A genus of 30 species of shrubby, evergreen perennials with robust, erect stems, sometimes fleshy, carrying tufts of large oblong to oval leaves at the stem ends.*

Dieffenbachia seguine

Dieffenbachia maculata

The tiny flowers are carried like those of arum, on a spadix within a narrow, arum-like spathe. The plant is very poisonous and sap should not be allowed into the mouth or eyes. One particular symptom of poisoning is speechlessness, hence the common name 'dumb cane'. They are attractive foliage plants for the conservatory or home. Propagate by cuttings of stem tips or by stem sections 6–8cm (2½–3in) long. These are taken from the lower, leafless stems and inserted horizontally into the rooting medium. Dieffenbachia was named for J. P. Dieffenbach (1790–1863), the Administrator of the Royal Palace Gardens at Schonbrunn in Vienna, Austria.

Species cultivated

D. amoena Giant dumb cane Tropical America
A robust plant, with stems reaching 1.5m (5ft) or more. Leaves are 30–40cm (12–16in), oblong and glossy dark green.

D. maculata (*D. picta*) Common dumb cane Brazil
Growing to 1m (3ft) or so tall. Leaves are up to 25cm (10in) long, oblong-elliptic to oval, green spotted and blotched with creamy-white. Many forms and cultivars are grown with various amounts of cream coloration. The leaves of *D.m.* 'Rudolph Roehrs' are almost completely pale yellow-green, showing the normal dark green only on the narrow edges and veins.

D. oerstedii Mexico and Costa Rica
This is a robust plant, with stems growing to 90cm (3ft) or more. The deep green leaves are oval to lance-shaped, often somewhat asymmetrically so. *D.o.* 'Variegata' has ivory-white midribs.

D. seguine Tropical America
One of the largest species, stems eventually attaining 2m (6½ft) or more in height. Leaves are variable, from oval to elliptic and lance-shaped, to 45cm (1½ft) long, glossy deep green, somewhat fleshy. Several variegated forms are known: 'Irrorata', very distinct in having a thinner-textured yellow-green leaf with dark green edges and blotches and whitish stalks; 'Lineata', green leaf but white-striped leaf stalks; 'Liturata', with a cream zone on either side of the midrib; 'Nobilis', spotted bright pale green.

DIOSCOREA

Dioscoreaceae
True yams

Origin: *Tropics and sub-tropics – widespread. A genus of at least 500 species of mainly herbaceous, tuberous or rhizomatous perennials with twining stems. Among their number are several species which are an important food crop in tropical countries. A much lesser number have ornamental foliage and are well worth trying in the home or conservatory. Propagate by dividing the rootstock, by cuttings of*

Dioscorea discolor

young basal shoots or by seed in spring. Dioscorea *honours Pedanios Dioscorides, the first-century Greek doctor, herbalist and author of the original* Materia Medica.

Species cultivated

D. discolor Ornamental yam Surinam
Stems on mature plants exceed 2m (6½ft) in height. Leaves are alternate, oval to heart shaped, 10–15cm (4–6in) long, velvety, olive-green with a pattern of silvery or silvery-pink veins above, and with purple beneath. It is one of the most handsome of the variegated-leaved yams.

DIZYGOTHECA

Araliaceae

Origin: *Australasia. A genus of 17 species of shrubs and small trees with alternate leaves having seven to 11 leaflets radiating out from the top of the stalk, which are often wavy-edged or lobed. The species described is the most commonly cultivated, making a decorative leafy plant for the home or conservatory, but best with additional humidity*

Dizygotheca elegantissima

in a dry room. Propagate by imported seed in warmth, by air-layering in spring and summer or by taking stem sections as cuttings. Dizygotheca *derives from the Greek* dis, *twice,* zygos, *a yoke and* thake, *a case, there being twice as many anther lobes as would be expected from the number of stamens.*

Species cultivated

D. elegantissima (*Aralia elegantissima*)
This erect, little branched shrub grows to 2m (6½ft), making a small tree in the wild. Leaves are long-stalked, with seven to ten very narrow, lance-shaped, deeply toothed leaflets reaching 15cm (6in) long by 1.5cm (⅝in) wide; when young they are a shining coppery-red becoming deep green as they mature. Flowers are not produced on pot plants. Large, flowering-sized specimens have much broader, stiffer leaflets.

DRACAENA
Agavaceae (Liliaceae)

Origin: *Tropical and sub-tropical Africa and Asia. A genus of 150 species of trees and shrubs with lance-shaped, leathery leaves growing either in tufts at the tips of the stems or more normally along the stem lengths, in the former case giving the plant a rather palm-like appearance. The flowers are small and rather insignificant and are carried in panicles or occasionally in heads or spikes. They are followed by often colourful berries. Dracaenas make attractive foliage plants for house or conservatory. Propagate by cuttings, either basal, tip or stem sections, in spring or summer in warmth, also by seed in warmth.*

Dracaena *derives from the Greek* drakaina, *a dragon, from the dragon tree* (D. draco) *of the Canary Islands.*

Species cultivated

D. angustifolia Solomon Islands
It can grow to 2m (6½ft) or more in a large container, but can easily be kept to half this. The stems are slender, branching and send out suckers. Leaves are 15–25cm (6–10in) long, narrowly lance-shaped and recurved, leathery-textured, and a glossy rich green. *D.a.* 'Honoriae', a graceful species deserving of wider recognition, has creamy-yellow leaf edges.

D. deremensis Tropical Africa
This is a slow-growing plant which can reach 3m (10ft) or more in a pot. Leaves grow to 45cm (1½ft) long by 5cm (2in) wide, sword-shaped, glossy green with faint longitudinal striping, usually erect, occasionally arching over. When the plant is small it will sometimes produce reddish flowers. *D.d.* 'Bausei' has two broad creamy-white

bands separated by a narrow greyish line; 'Warneckei' has green leaves with pale grey-green bands edged with yellow.

D. fragrans Corn plant Tropical Africa
Stems grow to 3m (10ft) in a pot, twice this in the open. Leaves are 60cm (2ft) or more long and 10cm (4in) wide, strap-shaped, gracefully arching over and down. The fragrant yellow flowers, when produced, are followed by orange-red fruits. *D.f.* 'Massangeana' has broad yellow and pale green central bands; 'Victoria' has a silvery grey-green central band bordered with creamy-yellow.

D. marginata Madagascar dragon tree Malagasy
Reaching a height of 1–2m (3–6½ft) in a pot, considerably more in the open, but always slow-growing. Leaves are 30–40cm (12–16in) long, very narrow, green edged with red, with a central vein of the same colour. It is very closely allied to *D. concinna* and *D. cincta* which may sometimes replace it in cultivation. *D.m.* 'Variegata' has cream-striped leaves; 'Tricolor' is similar, but with additional red edging to its leaves.

Left Dracaena angustifolia
Below Dracaena deremensis 'Bausei'

DRYNARIA
Polypodiaceae

Origin: *Old World tropics and Australia. A genus of about 20 species of ferns, most of which form rhizomes and are epiphytic, that is, they grow perched on another plant. Those described here are very effective in hanging baskets. Like the better known stag's horn fern* (Platycerium), *they produce two very distinct types of frond. The sterile fronds are stalkless and press fairly closely to their tree branch host, acting as collectors of dead leaves and other organic debris which then breaks down into humus and is invaded by the fern's roots. The fertile fronds are long-stalked, smooth-edged and pinnate to pinnatifid. Grown on a slab of rough bark, section of tree fern stem or in a basket, the ferns form compact mounds of overlapping sterile and gracefully arching fertile fronds, together creating a very pleasing composition. Propagate by spores or division in spring.* Drynaria *derives from the Greek* drys, *oak; the sterile leaves are rather like those of certain oaks.*

Drynaria quercifolia

Species cultivated
D. quercifolia Oak fern India, Malaysia, Australia
Rhizomes are thick, short and woody. Sterile fronds are 20–30cm (8–12in) long, oval and lobed. Fertile fronds grow to 60–90cm (2–3ft) long including the stalk, by 30cm (1ft) or more wide, and are deeply pinnatifid. Sporangia grow in two rows between the lateral veins of the pinnae.

EPISCIA
Gesneriaceae

Origin: *Tropical America and West Indies. A genus of 40 species of prostrate to trailing perennials with pairs of oval to elliptic leaves often patterned with white and gold and with a metallic sheen. They have tubular flowers opening to five flared, rounded lobes. They make fine hanging basket or pan plants for a conservatory or room if sufficient humidity can be provided. Propagate by division, by detaching plantlets growing upon the runners, or by cuttings, all in warmth in summer.* Episcia *derives from the Greek* episkios, *shaded, referring to their natural habitat.*

Species cultivated
E. cupreata Flame violet Colombia, Venezuela
A creeping or trailing plant, with stems growing to 40cm (16in) or more in length. Leaves are elliptic, slightly toothed, up to 6–8cm (2½–3in) long, their surfaces puckered or quilted, normally green

Above Episcia dianthiflora
Left Episcia cupreata

with a coppery flush and often having the veins picked out in silver, white or pink. Flowers are bright red, 2–2.5cm (¾–1in) wide, spotted with yellow within. Several named forms are available with varying silver variegation or a deeper coppery flush to the leaves.

E. dianthiflora Lace flower Mexico

Tufted at first, sending out creeping, hairy runners bearing small plantlets. Leaves are oval, with shallow, rounded teeth, growing to 4cm (1½in) long, thickish, dull green, with a purple midrib, softly and shortly downy above. Flowers are 2.5cm (1in), pure white with deeply fringed petals.

EXACUM

Gentianaceae

Origin: *Tropical Asia and India, islands of the Indian Ocean. A genus of 40 species of annuals, biennials and perennials with opposite, smooth-edged leaves and rounded flowers in clusters from the leaf axils. They are splendid flowering pot plants. Propagate by seed in spring, or for larger plants sow in autumn and these will flower earlier than spring-sown plants. Exacum derives from the Gaelic name* exacon, *a vernacular name for* Centaurium *and used by Linnaeus for this genus.*

Exacum affine

Species cultivated

E. affine Socotra (Indian Ocean)

A bushy annual or biennial, 15–25cm (6–10in) tall. The dark green leaves are broadly oval to elliptic, 1.5–4cm (⅝–1½in) long. Flowers are 1.5–2cm (⅝–¾in) across, five-petalled, purplish-blue, with yellow stamens; they open from summer to autumn.

FICUS
Moraceae
Figs

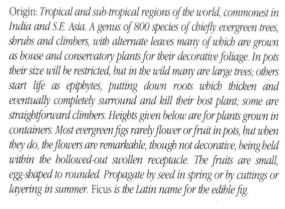

Origin: *Tropical and sub-tropical regions of the world, commonest in India and S.E. Asia. A genus of 800 species of chiefly evergreen trees, shrubs and climbers, with alternate leaves many of which are grown as house and conservatory plants for their decorative foliage. In pots their size will be restricted, but in the wild many are large trees; others start life as epiphytes, putting down roots which thicken and eventually completely surround and kill their host plant; some are straightforward climbers. Heights given below are for plants grown in containers. Most evergreen figs rarely flower or fruit in pots, but when they do, the flowers are remarkable, though not decorative, being held within the hollowed-out swollen receptacle. The fruits are small, egg-shaped to rounded. Propagate by seed in spring or by cuttings or layering in summer. Ficus is the Latin name for the edible fig.*

Below Ficus elastica
'Schrijveriana'
Bottom Ficus
microcarpa 'Hawaii'

Species cultivated

F. benjamina Weeping fig Tropical Asia
A large tree in the wild, but easily kept to 2m (6½ft) or so in a pot. Leaves are 5–10cm (2–4in) long, oval, tapering to a slender point, shining dark green on arching to hanging stems. Fruits are globe-shaped, 1–1.5cm (⅜–⅝in) wide, black and very decorative. For plants sold under the name 'Hawaii', see *F. microcarpa* 'Hawaii'.

F. elastica Rubber plant India, Malaysia
In pots it grows only to 2–3m (6½–10ft), but in the wild will make a tree up to 30m (100ft) tall or more; it is relatively slow-growing. Leaves are 15–30cm (6–12in) long, oblong to elliptic, rich glossy green with a paler central vein. Fruits are not produced on pot plants. 'Decora' is the commonly grown rubber plant with broader leaves than the type, tinted pinky-bronze when first opening. 'Doescheri' has leaves variegated with grey-green, creamy-yellow and white, the darkest colour near the pale veins; they also have pink stalks. 'Schrijveriana' is similar with somewhat broader leaves and red leaf stalks. 'Zulu Shield' has similar variegation with dark-red leaf stalks.

F. microcarpa (*F. nitida, F. retusa*) Laurel fig S.E. Asia and eastern Asia
Large shrub or small tree with the overall effect of *F. benjamina* as a pot specimen, but with blunt-pointed oval leaves. Makes an effective houseplant of 45–120cm (1½–4ft). 'Hawaii' is edged and splashed with creamy-white; almost always seen incorrectly named under *F. benjamina*.

F. nitida
A confusing name; officially a synonym of *F. benjamina* (*q.v.*), but also wrongly used for *F. microcarpa*.

*Fittonia verschaffeltii
argyroneura* 'Minima'

FITTONIA
Acanthaceae

Origin: *Peru. A genus of two species of creeping, evergreen perennials
with broad, decorative leaves having the veins marked in a
contrasting colour. Their small flower spikes add little to the display.
These plants need additional humidity in most homes and
conservatories. They grow well in terrariums, and can also be used
for hanging baskets. Propagate by careful division or by cuttings in
warmth in summer.* Fittonia *was named for Elizabeth and Sarah
Mary Fitton, who wrote* Conversations on Botany *in 1817.*

Species cultivated

F. argyroneura See *F. verschaffeltii argyroneura.*

F. verschaffeltii Painted net leaf, Nerve plant
A creeping to tufted plant, growing to 15cm (6in) tall. Leaves are oval,
7–10cm (2¾–4in) long, dark green with the veins picked out boldly in
red, forming an elaborate network over the leaf surface. Flowers are
small, reddish to yellowish and borne in short spikes.

F.v. argyroneura Silver net leaf
The most commonly seen form with the veining clearly marked in
white; a very decorative plant. *F.v.a.* 'Minima' is similar, but much
smaller, seldom exceeding 10cm (4in) in height, with leaves 2–3.5cm
(¾–1½in) long.

GERBERA
Compositae

Origin: *Africa, and Asia east to Bali. A genus of 70 species of
herbaceous perennials with leaves in rosettes and solitary flowers on
long stalks. The flowers of wild species have one or two rows of ray
florets. They are attractive flowering plants for the sunny conservatory*

Gerbera hybrid

or window sill and are best repropagated every two or three years to keep them compact. Gerberas are also very long-lasting as cut flowers. Propagate by seed, by division or by cuttings of non-flowering shoots, all in spring. Gerbera was named for Traugott Gerber (d. 1743), a German naturalist and traveller.

Species cultivated

G. jamesonii Barberton daisy South Africa
Clump-forming, with 25–40cm (10–16in) long, deeply pinnately lobed, oblong and spatula-shaped leaves, dull green above, white-woolly beneath. Flowers are 10cm (4in) wide, yellow to orange-red, on leafless stems growing to 45cm (1½ft) high.

Hybrids and seed strains

These come in a wide range of colours including red, pink, orange, yellow and white, many are double or semi-double.
'Happipot' is a dwarf seed strain 20–30cm (8–12in) high, bred especially for growing in pots. The flowers are semi-double to double and up to 8.5cm (3½in) across.

Opposite page
Guzmania sanguinea

GOMPHRENA
Amaranthaceae

Origin: *Tropics of Central and South America with outliers in S.E. Asia and Australia. A genus of 100 species of annuals, biennials and perennials with smooth-edged, opposite leaves and usually rounded heads of tiny flowers. The species described below can be grown in a pot in the conservatory or on a sunny window sill and has a very long season of flowering. Propagate by seed sown in early spring.* Gomphrena *is the Latin name for an unknown sort of amaranth.*

Gomphrena globosa

Species cultivated
G. globosa Globe amaranth Tropical Asia
Erect and much branched annual growing to 45cm (1½ft) tall. Leaves are 10cm (4in) long, oblong to elliptic, in opposite pairs. Flowers are tiny, almost hidden within the pink, purple, white, yellow or orange papery bracts, which together make up rounded to egg-shaped heads 2.5–4cm (1–1½in) long. 'Nana' or Dwarf Form is only 15cm (6in) tall.

GUZMANIA
Bromeliaceae

Origin: *Tropical America, West Indies. A genus of 110 species of evergreen rosette-forming perennials, the majority of which are epiphytic (that is, they grow perched on another plant). The leaves are strap-shaped and, as with many other bromeliads, overlap at their bases to form water-holding reservoirs. The three-petalled tubular flowers are yellow or white and carried in spikes or panicles often held within showy bracts. They are suitable for conservatory or home as long as some humidity is given. Propagate by offsets removed in late spring and summer.* Guzmania *commemorates Anastasio Guzman, an 18th-century Spanish naturalist.*

Species cultivated
G. sanguinea Costa Rica to Colombia and Ecuador
Leaves grow to 30cm (1ft) long, the outer ones are green, the inner of each rosette bright red with yellow-green centres. Flowers are 4cm
(*illustrated previous page*) (1½in) wide and almost stemless.

GYNURA
Compositae

Origin: *Africa to E. Asia and Malaysia. A genus of 100 species of evergreen perennials, shrubs and climbers with rather fleshy, alternate smooth-edged leaves and flower heads similar to groundsel. They make good pot plants, grown for their decorative leaves. Propagate by cuttings in late spring or summer.* Gynura *is derived from the Greek* gyne, *female and* oura, *a tail, referring to the long stigmas.*

Gynura 'Purple Passion'

Species cultivated

G. aurantiaca Velvet plant Java

An erect, soft shrub, up to 90cm (3ft) tall, becoming partially climbing with age, and then growing to 3m (10ft). Stems and leaves are densely clothed with velvety violet-purple hairs. Leaves are 10–20cm (4–8in) long, oval to elliptic, coarsely double-toothed. Flowers are 1.5–2cm (⅝–¾in) wide, orange-yellow, with age becoming purple; they are carried in loose corymbs in winter.

G. 'Purple Passion'

A hybrid, probably between *G. aurantiaca* and *G. sarmentosa*, with semi-twining stems. Leaves growing to 11cm (4½in) long, lance-shaped to narrowly oblong, purple-hairy, with lobed and toothed edges, purplish-green above, deep red-purple beneath.

HIPPEASTRUM

Amaryllidaceae

Origin: *Central and South America. A genus of 75 species of bulbous plants with tufts of strap-shaped leaves and bold six-petalled,*

Hippeastrum × *ackermannii*
'Red Lion'

funnel-shaped, lily-like flowers on erect, leafless stems. They are suitable for home or conservatory, and need to be dried off when the leaves begin to turn yellow in summer. Propagate by offsets or by seed sown in spring in warmth. If kept without a dry resting period the seedlings will mature and flower more quickly, but must then be rested after flowering. Hippeastrum *derives from the Greek* equus, *a horse and* hippeus, *rider, because the flower buds within their spathes supposedly suggest a horse and rider.*

Species cultivated

H. × ackermannii (*H. × acramanii*) Amaryllis
This name covers the popular large-flowered hybrid cultivars derived from *H. aulicum, H. elegans, H. reginae, H. reticulatum* and *H. striatum*, now so freely available in garden centres and multiple stores. They are vigorous plants with thick-textured, dark green leaves to 60cm (2ft) long and robust flowering stems 45–60cm (1½–2ft) or more tall, having umbels of two to four huge lily-like flowers in shades of red, pink, orange and white, sometimes striped, which open either just before or with the young leaves in late winter or spring. Both named cultivars and un-named seedlings are commercially available.

Howeia forsterana

HOWEIA (HOWEA)
Palmae

Origin: *Lord Howe Island, S.E. Pacific. A genus of two species of palm, growing to 20m (65ft) in the wild, having erect stems bearing arching, pinnate leaves. They make very good pot or tub plants when small. Propagate by seed in spring in heat.* Howeia *was named after Lord Howe Island where they are found.*

Species cultivated

H. belmoreana (*Kentia belmoreana*) Curly palm, Sentry palm
Growing to 2–3m (6½–10ft) tall in pots. Leaves are 1m (3ft), strongly arching, short-stalked; leaflets very narrow and lance-shaped, pointed outwards.

H. forsterana (*Kentia forsterana*) Kentia palm, Sentry palm, Thatchleaf palm, Paradise palm
Growing to 2–3m (6½–10ft) tall in pots. Leaves are less strongly arching, long-stalked, with leaflets that are very narrow and lance-shaped, pointed downwards.

HYPOESTES
Acanthaceae

Origin: *Tropical Africa and Asia, especially Malagasy. A genus of 40 to 150 species (depending upon the botanical authority consulted). It comprises evergreen shrubs, sub-shrubs and perennials with opposite pairs of undivided leaves sometimes colourfully variegated, and spike-like clusters of tubular, two-lipped flowers growing at the ends of the stems. The species described is a popular pot plant. Propagate by cuttings from spring to late summer or by seed in spring.* Hypoestes *derives from the Greek* hypo, *under and* estia, *a house, a slightly obscure reference to the way the floral calyces are covered by bracts.*

Hypoestes phyllostachya

Species cultivated

H. phyllostachya Polka dot plant, Freckle face Malagasy

A sub-shrubby perennial growing to 60cm (2ft) in height, but kept to less if pruned annually. Leaves are up to 6cm (2½in) long, oval, deep green, freckled with small, irregular pink spots. Flowers about 2cm (¾in) long, lavender, borne singly from the leaf axils. *H.p.* 'Splash' is a selected form with larger, brighter leaf spots. *H. phyllostachya* was for long mis-identified as *H. sanguinolenta*, an allied species with leaves veined, not spotted, red.

IMPATIENS

Balsaminaceae

Origin: *Warm temperate and tropical Africa and Asia, also Europe and a few hardy species in North America. A genus of about 600 species of annuals, perennials and soft shrubs, most of which have fleshy, rather succulent stems, undivided, often toothed leaves and distinctive asymmetrical flowers. These have three, occasionally five, small sepals, one of which has a petal-like spur, and five petals, the*

Impatiens walleriana 'Variegata'

Impatiens 'New Guinea Hybrid'

upper one often hooded. The other four unite into pairs which are often deeply lobed. Those described are splendid plants for home and conservatory. Propagate by cuttings taken from spring to late summer, or by seed in spring. Impatiens *derives from the Latin for* impatient; *the seed capsules open explosively when ripe.*

Species cultivated

I. × New Guinea Hybrids See under *I. schlechteri*.

I. schlechteri New Guinea

A shrubby perennial growing to 60cm (2ft) or more, but easily maintained at half this height in containers. Leaves are oval to lance-shaped, 5–10cm (2–4in) long, toothed, glossy rich green and often flushed with red, carried in whorls of three to seven. Flowers are bright red, pink or orange, flat, about 4.5cm (1¾in) wide with pale slender spurs of equal length. They open from spring to autumn. This species is not common in cultivation, but is one parent of the new race known as New Guinea Hybrids. These can have green, red or bronze leaves, usually variegated with an irregular, yellow, mid-vein stripe. The glistening flowers range from shades of red to orange, pink, purple and white. Tropical.

I. sultanii See *I. walleriana*.

I. walleriana (*I. holstii;* now including *I. sultanii*) Buzy Lizzie, Patient Lucy Tanzania, Mozambique

A shrubby perennial growing to 60cm (2ft) or more tall. Leaves are 4–10cm (1½–4in) long, lance-shaped to oval. Flowers are 3–5cm (1¼–2in) across, flat, with a 4cm (1½in) spur, scarlet, orange, purple, magenta, pink or white. They will open throughout the year if temperatures are kept above 13°C (56°F).

Kohleria digitaliflora

KOHLERIA
Gesneriaceae

Origin: *Mexico, Central America and northern South America. A genus of 50 species of shrubs and perennials growing from scaly rhizomes. Their leaves are lance-shaped to oval, borne in whorls or pairs and the flowers are tubular with five rounded lobes carried singly or in clusters from the upper leaf axils. They make very handsome pot plants. Keep them barely moist but not dry during the winter and re-pot annually in spring, separating the scaly rhizome and discarding the rest of the plant. Propagate in the same way or by seed if available. Kohleria was named for Michael Kohler, 19th-century Swiss teacher of natural history.*

Species cultivated
K. digitaliflora Colombia
A herbaceous plant. Stems are covered with white hairs, robust, erect and growing to 60cm (2ft) or more. Leaves are elliptic and lance-shaped to oval, up to 20cm (8in) in length, hairy, dark green with shallow, rounded teeth. Flowers are 3cm (1¼in) long, white and

pink, densely covered with white hairs, petal lobes green with purple spots, borne in stalked clusters of up to six from the upper leaf axils in summer to autumn.

MARANTA

Marantaceae

Origin: *Tropical America. A genus of about 20 species of clump-forming perennials growing from rhizomes. They have undivided leaves with sheathing stalks. The flowers are small and three-petalled with two larger petal-like staminodes, but are mostly not showy, the plants usually being grown for their decorative foliage. Arrowroot is obtained from the roots of M. arundinacea. They are excellent house and warm conservatory plants. Propagate by division when potting, or by cuttings with two or three leaves in summer in warmth. Maranta was named for Bartolommeo Maranti, an Italian physician and botanist living in Venice in 1559.*

Species cultivated

M. kerchoviana See *M. leuconeura*

M. leuconeura Prayer plant Brazil
Stems are short, usually branched and spreading, eventually reaching a height of 30cm (1ft) Leaves are 15cm (6in) long, elliptic to oblong, usually blunt, green.

M.l. erythroneura (*M. tricolor*) Herringbone plant
Dark green veins with a silvery central zone and crimson veins curving to the edges of the leaf.

M.l. kerchoveana Rabbit tracks/foot
Light green leaves and a row of dark greenish-brown blotches between the veins.

M.l. leuconeura (*M.l. massangeana*)
Dark green veins with a silvery central zone and vein patterning of the same colour.

Maranta leuconeura erythroneura

MONSTERA
Araceae

Origin: *Tropical America. A genus of 25 species of evergreen root climbers many of which are epiphytic (that is, they grow perched on another plant) in the wild. They have alternate, long-stalked leaves, which can be oval to oblong, and tiny petalless flowers carried on a spadix within a spathe typical of members of the arum family. They are familiar pot plants in conservatory or home, tolerant of poor light and a dry atmosphere, but looking much more healthy and attractive where humidity is provided. They grow particularly well on a moss stick. Propagate by stem tip or leaf bud cuttings in warmth in summer.* Monstera *may be derived from the Latin* monstrifer, *monster-bearing, referring to its large, oddly perforated leaves, but this is by no means certain.*

Monstera deliciosa 'Variegata'

Species cultivated
M. deliciosa (*M. pertusa, Philodendron pertusum*) Ceriman, Swiss cheese plant, Mexican bread fruit Mexico to Central America
A very tall climber in warm countries, but rarely more than 2–3m (6–10ft) in a pot. Leaves are 40–90cm (16–36in) long, broadly oval, the edges of which are deeply cleft, leaving curved, blunt-ended oblong lobes; on mature plants they are also perforated with large elliptic to oblong holes. Spathes grow to 20cm (8in) or more long, creamy-white or green. Fruits are egg-shaped, with a pineapple-like scent; they are edible but contain minute spicules which can prove an irritant to sensitive throats. *M.d.* 'Variegata' has variable yellowish-green markings, but is unstable and very liable to revert to dark green.

MUSA
Musaceae

Origin: *Tropical Asia and East Africa. A genus of 25 species of evergreen perennials, including the familiar, edible banana. They have trunk-like stems made up of sheathing leaf stalks closely wrapped around each other, and very large, oblong to elliptic leaves. The spike-like inflorescences are made up of many six-tepalled flowers often with five fused and one free tepal, and carried within sometimes colourful bracts. The typical banana fruits are, correctly, cylindrical berries. They can be grown in the home and conservatory mainly as foliage plants when young, but some species will flower in a tub, and* M. × paradisiaca *'Dwarf Cavendish' will fruit if given adequate space. Propagate by division, offsets or suckers when potting, or by seed of the species sown in warmth in spring.* Musa *is probably derived from*

Musa × paradisiaca

the Arabic common name mouz or moz for the banana, though it is
sometimes said to be for Antonius Musa (63–14BC), Physician to the
Roman Emperor Octavius Augustus.

Species cultivated

M. cavendishii See under *M. × paradisiaca*.

M. × paradisiaca (*M. × sapientum*) Common banana
A hybrid between *M. acuminata* and *M. balbisiana* which includes
the cultivars of dessert and cooking bananas and is very like the
parent species. *M. × p.* 'Dwarf Cavendish' (*M. cavendishii*, Canary
Island banana) is the most rewarding banana plant to grow for fruit,
being a dwarf mutant growing to about 2–2.5m (6½–8ft), flowering
and fruiting in a large tub if given room to reach its mature size.

M. × sapientum See *M. × paradisiaca*.

NEMATANTHUS
(inc. HYPOCYRTA)

Gesneriaceae

Origin: *South America; those listed below all from Brazil. A genus of
about 30 species of shrubs and perennials, which are largely epiphytic
and grow perched on another plant. They are evergreen, with pairs of
undivided leaves closely set on semi-erect to prostrate stems. The
flowers are tubular, in many species the lower side of the upper half is
inflated to look like a pelican's pouch and constricted to a small*

Nematanthus gregarius

mouth ringed with five tiny lobes. The species described make splendid hanging basket plants. Nematanthus *derives from the Greek* nema, *a thread and* anthos, *a flower; several species have long flower stalks allowing the blooms to dangle beneath the leaves.*

Species cultivated
N. gregarius (*N. radicans, Hypocyrta radicans*)
Stems are trailing, and 30–60cm (1–2ft) long. Leaves grow in pairs or whorls of three, 2–4cm (¾–1¼in) long, somewhat fleshy but firm, dark lustrous green. Flowers on short stalks, 2cm (¾in) long, orange with yellow lobes.

N. radicans See *N. gregarius.*

NICODEMIA
Loganiaceae

Origin: *Sri Lanka, Mascarene Islands. A genus of six species of shrubs formerly included in the genus* Buddleja, *but separated on the basis of fleshy, berry-like fruits (those of* Buddleja *are dry capsules). The species described here make showy tub or border plants for the conservatory or large room. Propagate by cuttings in late summer, or by seed in spring or when ripe.* Nicodemia *honours Gaetano Nicodemo (d. 1803), Italian botanist and curator of the Lyons Botanic Garden 1799–1803 when he committed suicide.*

Species cultivated
N. madagascariensis (*Buddleja madagascariensis*) Malagasy
An erect growing plant which reaches 2–3m (6½–10ft) or more in height. Leaves are lance-shaped growing to 13cm (5in) in length, dark green above, white-felted beneath. Flowers are small, bright orange and borne in slenderly pyramid-shaped panicles at the ends of the stems from winter to spring. Fruits are purple.

Nicodemia madagascariensis

PACHYSTACHYS

Acanthaceae

Origin: *Tropical America. A genus of five or six species of shrubs and evergreen perennials closely related to* Jacobinia. *They have opposite pairs of smooth-edged leaves and tubular flowers with very unequal lobes which are borne in twos and threes within large bracts, many together making spike-like clusters or heads. They make very good pot plants. Propagate by cuttings in summer.* Pachystachys *derives from the Greek* pachys, *thick and* stachys, *a spike.*

Pachystachys lutea

Species cultivated

P. lutea Lollipop-plant Peru
A shrub reaching a height of 1m (3ft) or more. Leaves grow to 10–18cm (4–7in) long, lance-shaped to narrowly oval, the upper surface a glossy dark green. Flowers grow to 4–5cm (1½–2in) long, white, within golden-yellow bracts, making up flower spikes reaching 10cm (4in) long from late spring to autumn.

PANDANUS

Pandanaceae
Screw pines

Origin: *Tropical Africa, Asia, Australasia mostly on sea coasts and islands. A genus of 600 to 650 species of evergreen trees, shrubs and climbers, often distinctive in the wild because of their prop roots, which support the erect stem and branches. The leaves are usually crowded near the stem tips and arranged spirally giving them their common name of screw pine. The leaves are strap-shaped and of thick texture, often with finely spiny edges. The single sex flowers are petalless, the males are carried in branched spikes, the females in rounded heads which develop into tight cone shaped clusters of fruits. They are attractive pot or tub plants, though care must be taken in handling and siting those with prickle-edged leaves.* Pandanus *is a Latinized form of the Malaysian name* pandan.

Species cultivated

P. sanderi Reputedly from Timor, Indonesia
Eventually reaching 2m (6½ft) or more, but slow-growing. Leaves are 45–75cm (1½–2½ft) long, very narrow with minute spiny teeth, rich green with a yellow central stripe.
P. veitchii Polynesia
Stem is short, freely branching when well established, growing to 2m (6½ft) or more tall. Leaves are arching, 60–90cm (2–3ft) long with wide creamy-white edges which are spiny.

(illustrated overleaf)

Pandanus sanderi

PASSIFLORA
Passifloraceae
Passion flowers

Passiflora coccinea

Origin: *Chiefly from the Americas, but a few species from Asia and Australia. A genus of 400 or more species of climbing plants, with alternate, often three- to five-lobed leaves, holding on to their supports by means of tendrils. The flowers are usually solitary, growing from the upper leaf axils, and are followed by rounded to egg-shaped berries which are sometimes edible. The flowers are large and often showy, tubular at the base, with ten tepals which can be spread out flat or overlapped to form a bowl-like shape. The ovary with its three styles and five stamens are borne together on a central stalk (androphore) which is surrounded by one or several rows of fleshy filaments forming a corona. Passion flowers can be grown against the back wall of a conservatory, or trained around and up a wire or stick. When young some are successful houseplants, blooming when very small. Propagate by cuttings in summer with bottom heat, or by seed when ripe or in spring in warmth.* Passiflora *derives from the Latin* passio, *passion and* flos, *a flower, from the interpretation of the flower by Jesuit missionaries to South America.*

Species cultivated
P. coccinea Red passion flower, Red granadilla Venezuela to Bolivia and Brazil

Stems are slender, slightly angled, red-downy, growing to 4m (13ft) or more. The toothed leaves are broadly oblong to disk-shaped, 6–13cm (2½–5in) long. Flowers are 8cm (3in) or more wide, scarlet, with crimson, pink and white outer filaments 2cm (¾in) long and shorter inner white ones. The edible fruits are egg-shaped, about 5cm (2in) long, orange or yellow with six green stripes.

P. edulis Passion fruit, Purple granadilla Brazil (cultivated in warmer countries)
Stems grow to 3m (10ft) or more. Leaves are deeply three-lobed, toothed, reaching 10cm (4in) or more across. Flowers are 5–7cm (2–2¾in) wide, white, the corona of white filaments tipped with purple. They are followed by 5cm (2in) long egg-shaped fruits which are greenish-yellow to purplish.

Passiflora edulis

PELLIONIA
Urticaceae

Origin: *Tropical Asia and Polynesia. A genus of about 50 species of low-growing perennials with alternate leaves usually all lying on one plane, and small insignificant flowers. They are fine foliage plants for the conservatory and home and can be grown in pots, pans and hanging baskets. Propagate by division or by cuttings taken in late spring and summer.*

Pellionia *was named for Adolphe Odet Pellion (1796–1868), a French Admiral who accompanied Louis Freycinet on a voyage around the world.*

Pellionia daveauana

Species cultivated
P. daveauana (*P. repens*) Trailing water-melon begonia Burma, Vietnam, Malaysia
Stems are rather succulent and up to 60cm (2ft) long. Leaves are 2.5–5cm (1–2in) long, broadly elliptic, asymmetrical at the base and somewhat fleshy; their upper surfaces are bronze to olive green with purple-suffused edges and a broad, paler green band along the centre of each leaf.

PERISTROPHE
Acanthaceae

Origin: *Tropical Africa and Asia. A genus of about 15 species of perennials and sub-shrubs with opposite smooth-edged leaves and tubular flowers that grow in clusters. Propagate by cuttings in summer.*

Peristrophe *derives from the Greek* peri, *around and* strophe, *to twist, from the twisted corolla lobes.*

Peristrophe hyssopifolia
'Aureo-Variegata'

Species cultivated

P. angustifolia See *P. hyssopifolia.*

P. hyssopifolia (*P. angustifolia*) Java

This plant is widely spreading, with stems 60–90cm (2–3ft) long. Leaves are 5–8cm (2–3in) long, narrowly elliptic to lance-shaped, dark green. Flowers are small, red-purple, within two oval bracts, one larger than the other, opening in summer. *P.h.* 'Aureo-Variegata' is an attractive foliage plant. Its leaves have a central yellow zone and veins that create a feathery pattern.

P. speciosa India

Evergreen shrub reaching a height of 60–90cm (2–3ft). Leaves 10–13cm (4–5in) long, oval to elliptic, slender-pointed. The violet-purple flowers are about 4cm (1½in) long, showy, tubular in shape, the lobes fused into two equal-sized lips. They are borne in clusters from the upper leaf axils in winter.

PHILODENDRON

Araceae

Philodendron erubescens

Origin: *Tropical Central and South America. A genus of 200 or more species of evergreen shrubs and climbers, of which many are epiphytic (in the wild they grow on another plant). Many have a distinct juvenile phase with leaves quite dissimilar to those of mature plants; plants grown in pots are often at this earlier stage of growth. They have arrow- to heart-shaped, often leathery leaves of a dark glossy green which are alternate on climbing species, crowded or in rosettes on free-standing ones. Their flowers are small and are borne, typically of the arum family, on small spadices partly surrounded by white, green or red spathes. The plants are suitable for the home or conservatory, the climbing ones needing support, ideally of a moss stick. Propagate by cuttings of young tips, stem sections or leaf buds, all in summer.* Philodendron *derives from the Greek* philo, *love and* dendron, *a tree.*

Species cultivated

P. andreanum See *P. melanochrysum.*

P. 'Burgundy' A hybrid with slowly climbing stems. Leaves are to 30cm (1ft) long, triangular to lance-shaped, flushed with red above, the undersides and the winged leaf-stalks being a rich wine-red.

P. cordatum Heart-leaf S. Brazil

Stems are climbing. Leaves reach a length of 30–45cm (1–1½ft), oval to heart-shaped, the basal lobes touching or overlapping, much confused in cultivation with *P. scandens oxycardium.*

P. erubescens Blushing philodendron Trinidad, Colombia and Venezuela

Stems are climbing, red-purple when young. Leaves grow to 25cm

Philodendron scandens

(10in) long, oval to triangular, dark green with a strong coppery flush beneath.

P. ilsemannii Brazil

Leaves are narrowly triangular-oblong, arrowhead-shaped, creamy-white marbled with grey and dark green.

P. melanochrysum (*P. andreanum*) Black gold/Velour philodendron Colombia

Stems are climbing. Leaves grow to 45–75cm (1½–2½ft) in length, broadly arrow-shaped with a heart-shaped base, dark olive-green with an iridescent coppery gloss and paler veins.

P. oxycardium See under *P. scandens.*

P. scandens Heart leaf, Sweetheart plant Tropical America

Stems are climbing. Leaves are 10–15cm (4–6in) when juvenile, reaching 30cm (12in) when mature, oval, heart-shaped at the base, slender pointed, dark green with a silky sheen, sometimes flushed purple-red beneath.

P.s. oxycardium

The commonest philodendron grown as a houseplant, with leaves glossy green above and below.

PHOENIX

Palmae
Date palms

Origin: *Tropical and sub-tropical Africa and Asia. A genus of 17 species of palms, the stems terminating in rosettes of narrowly pinnate leaves, with the lowest leaflets often spine-like. The flowers are small and of single sex on individual plants, borne in dense panicles carried amongst the leaves. They are followed by fleshy fruits each containing a single, grooved seed. When young, date palms make useful and decorative pot plants. Propagate by seed sown in spring at not less than 21°C (70°F), or by suckers if available treated as cuttings and grown on in warmth.* Phoenix *is the Greek common name for the date palm.*

Species cultivated

P. roebelenii Pygmy date palm Assam to Vietnam
Eventually reaching 2–4m (6–13ft), sometimes producing suckers. Leaves are arching, 1–1.2m (3–4ft) long, flat and feathery with dark, glossy-green leaflets. Flowers grow in panicles to 45cm (1½ft) long, followed by egg-shaped black fruits which are 1.2cm (½in) long. Grows best at tropical temperatures with extra humidity.

Phoenix roebelenii

Piper ornatum

PIPER

Piperaceae
Peppers

Origin: *Pantropical. Depending upon the botanical authority consulted, a genus of 1,000 to 2,000 species of climbers, shrubs and small trees. They have alternate, undivided, often oval or heart-shaped leaves, in some cases beautifully marbled with white, pink, purple or red. The tiny, petalless, insignificant flowers are borne in cylindrical spikes and are followed by more or less fleshy, berry-like drupes. Propagate by cuttings in summer or by seed in spring.* Piper *derives from the Greek* peperi, *itself derived from an Indian name for pepper (*P. nigrum*).*

Species cultivated

P. crocatum (*P. ornatum crocatum*) Ornamental pepper Peru
A climbing plant, with wiry stems reaching 2–3m (6½–10ft) in length if planted out. Leaves are heart-shaped, the stalk seeming to join beneath as opposed to at the edge of the leaf. They are 8–13cm (3–5in) long, lustrous dark olive-green with bands of silver-pink dots along the veins, and deep purple beneath.

P. ornatum Celebes
Much like *P. crocatum,* but its leaves are relatively broader and more evenly marbled with silvery-pink which with age becomes white.

PLATYCERIUM

Polypodiaceae

Origin: *Africa, Australia, Malaysia, South America. A genus of 17 species of large, evergreen ferns of a uniquely imposing appearance, which in the wild grow perched on another plant (epiphytically). They have leathery fronds of two types, sterile and fertile. The sterile ones*

Platycerium bifurcatum

are usually simple, overlapping each other and pressed firmly against their support (a tree branch in the wild). Dead leaves and other organic debris collects behind them, decaying down to provide a nutritious humus. In the home or conservatory it is worthwhile inserting a little peaty compost to take the place of this natural humus supply. The fertile fronds are in most, but not all, species branched like those of a deer or elk horn, either arching, hanging down, or erect. Brown sporangia completely cover discrete areas of the undersides of the fertile frond lobes. The common stag's horn fern (P. bifurcatum) is a proven houseplant and the other species described here are worth trying in the home. All are easily grown in the warm conservatory. Propagate by spores or division in spring. A bromeliad-type compost gives the best results and these ferns can be grown in hanging baskets or, more effectively, pinned to slabs of tree bark or tree fern stem. Platycerium derives from the Greek platys, broad and keros, a horn, alluding to the shape of the fronds.

Species cultivated

P. alcicorne See *P. bifurcatum.*

P. bifurcatum (*P. alcicorne*) Common stag's horn fern Eastern Australia to Polynesia

Sterile fronds are rounded to kidney-shaped, wavy or slightly lobed, downy when young, reaching a width of 15–30cm (6–12in). The bright green fertile fronds are spreading to drooping, wedge-shaped at the base, repeatedly forking and diverging into several narrow lobes above. A very variable species with several distinctive forms described as cultivars: 'Majus' is somewhat larger with erect, brighter green fertile fronds; 'Netherlands' (*P. alcicorne* 'Regina Wilhelmina') has grey-green fronds which tend to be shorter and broader and radiate in all directions; and 'Ziesenherne' is smaller.

POLYPODIUM
Polypodiaceae

Origin: *Cosmopolitan. A genus once including over 1,000 species of fern, but now reduced by modern botanists to 75. They are ground-dwelling and epiphytic in growth (existing perched on another plant) and mostly evergreen, with branched rhizomes and usually pinnate or pinnately lobed fronds, though a few species have almost smooth-edged fronds. The spores on the undersides of the fronds have no coverings (indusia). Propagate by cuttings of rhizomes, division or spores in spring.* Polypodium *derives from the Greek* polys, *many and* podium, *a foot, referring to the branched rhizomes.*

Polypodium aureum

Species cultivated

P. aureum (*Phlebodium aureum*) Hare's foot fern Florida to Argentina and Australia
Epiphytic or ground dwelling with thick, creeping rhizomes densely covered by hair-like red-brown scales. Fronds are long-stalked and pinnatifid, reaching 30–90cm (1–3ft) or more in length, the lobes strap-shaped, waved and pointed, pale to yellow-green.

POLYSCIAS
Araliaceae

Origin: *Tropical Asia and Polynesia. A genus of 80 or so species which have also been classified in Aralia. They are distinctive foliage plants having alternate leaves which are usually shaped like outspread hands or pinnate, and umbels of small, greenish flowers each made up of four to eight perianth segments, but these are, however, seldom produced on potted specimens. Propagate by stem tip cuttings or by leafless sections of stems in summer.* Polyscias *derives from the Greek* polys, *many and* skias, *a sunshade or canopy, referring to the flowering umbels.*

Polyscias filicifolia

Species cultivated

P. filicifolia Fern-leaf aralia Polynesia

Shrub growing to 1m (3ft) or so, reaching 2.5m (8ft) in the open. Leaves are 30cm (1ft) long, pinnately divided, the leaf-lobes themselves are cleft and spiny-toothed, and bright green with purplish midribs when young. Mature specimens have broader, less toothed leaflets.

PSEUDERANTHEMUM

Acanthaceae

Origin: *Tropics – widespread. Depending upon the botanical authority, a genus of 60 to 120 species of shrubs and perennials very closely allied to* Eranthemum. *Several species have long been popular conservatory plants and can be cultivated successfully in the home. Some are best as foliage plants, others for their flowers. Erect to spreading in habit, they have opposite pairs of mainly undivided leaves, and flowers with slender tubes and five prominent petal lobes. Propagate by cuttings in spring or summer.*

Pseuderanthemum *derives from the Greek word* pseudo, *false and the allied* Eranthemum.

Species cultivated

P. atropurpureum (*Eranthemum atropurpureum*) Probably Polynesia, but naturalized in tropical America

Of shrubby erect habit, reaching 1.2m (4ft) in height if not regularly pruned. Leaves are oval to elliptic, 10–15cm (4–6in) long, usually strongly flushed with purple, but sometimes green or patterned with yellow, pink, white and green. Flowers are white or purple-flushed with a red-purple eye, about 2cm (¾in) wide, growing in short axillary spikes at the ends of the stems in summer. *P.a.* 'Tricolor' has deep purple leaves irregularly splashed with white, pink and green.

Below right
Pseuderanthemum reticulatum
Below *Pseuderanthemum atropurpureum* 'Tricolor'

P. reticulatum (*Eranthemum reticulatum*) Probably Polynesia, but widely grown and naturalized throughout the tropics
An erect, shrubby plant, reaching 90cm (3ft) or more in height. Leaves are narrowly oval to lance-shaped, 10–25cm (4–10in) long, rich green with an elaborate network of bright yellow veins. Flowers are 2.5cm (1in) or more wide, white with a red-purple throat and spotting on the lower petal, in small panicles at the ends of the stems in summer. *P.r.* 'Eldorado' has oval leaves and makes a more substantial foliage pot plant.

RHIPSALIDOPSIS
Cactaceae

Origin: *Brazil. A genus of two species of woody-based, somewhat shrubby cacti, which are epiphytic (that is, they grow perched on another plant in the wild). They have leafless stems which are branched and jointed. Between the joints they are flattened and appear leaf-like. The flowers are tubular at the base, the many narrow tepals opening to a wide, funnel-shaped bloom, the stigmas having narrow, spreading lobes. They make particularly rewarding hanging basket plants. Propagate by cuttings, taking pieces with one to three joints, preferably putting three cuttings around a 7.5cm (3in) pot and growing them together to make more of a display than a single shoot can.* Rhipsalidopsis *derives from the genus name* Rhipsalis *and the Greek* opsis, *like, referring to the resemblances between the genera.*

Species cultivated
R. gaertneri (*Schlumbergera gaertneri, Epiphyllopsis gaertneri*) Easter cactus
Stems are spreading and eventually hanging, forming a plant 20–30cm (8–12in) high. The stems are leaf-like in shape between nodes, each internode is 4–8cm (1½–3in) long, edged with shallow,

Rhipsalidopsis gaertneri

rounded teeth, purplish-green, carrying minute areoles with a few white bristles. The bright scarlet flowers are 6–9cm (2½–3½in) wide, with long, narrow tepals ending in a point, opening in spring.

R. rosea

Growing to 15cm (6in) high and wide, with hanging stems. The stems are leaf-like in shape between nodes, each internode is 2.5–4cm (1–1½in) long, edged with shallow, rounded teeth, green but sometimes flushed with red margins. Flowers are 3–4cm (1¼–1½in) wide, rose-pink to magenta-pink, very freely borne in late spring and early summer. A rewarding houseplant.

RUELLIA
Acanthaceae

Origin: *Tropics and sub-tropics, and North America. A genus of about 250 species of perennials and shrubs, split up into several genera by some botanists, but here considered as one. They have narrowly oblong to oval leaves in opposite pairs and tubular to funnel-shaped flowers opening to five broad, spreading lobes at the mouth, borne in spikes or singly in the axils of the upper leaves. Propagate by division if possible, by cuttings with bottom heat in spring, or by seed also with heat in spring. Ruellia was named for Jean Ruel (1475–1537), a French physician and herbalist serving King François I.*

Ruellia mackoyana

Species cultivated

R. devosiana Brazil

Sub-shrubby, producing spreading stems 20–45cm (8–18in) in height. Leaves grow up to 8cm (3in) long, narrowly elliptic, with velvety hairs, the upper surface a deep green bearing a white vein pattern, the lower surface purple. Flowers are 4cm (1½in) in length, white, the throat lilac and sometimes with streakings of the same colour elsewhere.

R. mackoyana Monkey plant Brazil

In size, habit and foliage, much like *R. devosiana,* but with bright carmine to purple-red flowers.

SAINTPAULIA
Gesneriaceae
African violets

Origin: *East Africa, most from one mountain range in Tanzania. A genus of 21 species of evergreen herbaceous perennials which form rosettes or are tufted; some are stemless, others have long stems. Their leaves are oval to almost round, often heart-shaped and scalloped at the edges and usually with short and long hairs on the leaf surface.*

The flowers are shortly tubular, opening to five lobes, and can be blue, violet, pink, red or white in colour. Until the early 1970s most cultivars were forms of S. ionantha and were typically rosetted stemless plants with single or double flowers. During the last fifteen or so years other species have been hybridized with it, bringing in the long-stemmed character that has resulted in the hanging and trailing cultivars, while smaller species have been used to develop a race of mini African violets. All of these will make excellent house and warm conservatory plants. Propagate by leaf cuttings in summer, species only also by seed in warmth in spring. Saintpaulia was named for Baron Walter von Saint Paul Illaire (1860–1910), who discovered the first species of this genus.

Saintpaulia *pendula*

Species cultivated

S. ionantha Coastal Tanzania
Rosette-forming and often growing in clumps. Leaves are 4–6cm (1½–2½in) long, long stalked, broadly oval to rounded, somewhat fleshy-textured with silky hairs. Flowers are 2–2.5cm (¾–1in) across and held above the leaves on long scapes 5–10cm (2–4in) tall, blue, violet, pink, red and white, blooming intermittently throughout the year. Very many cultivars have been raised.
S. pendula Tanzania (Usambara Mts.)
Similar to *S. ionantha,* but with elongating stems and solitary blue-purple flowers with darker throats.

SCHLUMBERGERA

Cactaceae

Origin: *Brazil. A genus of two species of cacti, which are epiphytic (growing perched on another plant in the wild) and allied to* Rhipsalidopsis. *They are sometimes still known as* Zygocactus. *They have thin green stems flattened into conspicuously jointed leaf-like segments which have toothed edges and small, bristly areoles. The tubular flowers are solitary or in pairs from the ends of the stems, having petals which are bent back rather abruptly and protruding stamens. All are excellent house and conservatory plants, particularly effective in hanging baskets. Propagate by cuttings of one or two stem sections in summer.* Schlumbergera *was named for Frederick Schlumberger, a Belgian horticulturalist of the late nineteenth century.*

Species cultivated
S. × bridgesii See *S. × buckleyi.*
S. × buckleyi (*S. × bridgesii*) Christmas cactus
A hybrid reaching a height of 30cm (1ft) with arching branches, the stem segments growing to 5cm (2in) long by 2.5cm (1in) wide,

Schlumbergera truncata

rounded at the ends with shallow rounded teeth. Flowers are 5.5–6.5cm (2⅕–2⅔in) long, the petals bending back at the mouth, magenta to rosy-purple, opening in winter. Several named cultivars are now commercially available, the following being recommended: 'Bicolor' (shades of rose-red), 'Joanne' (red with a purple throat), 'Noris' (red and purple), 'Weinachtesfreude' (pale and dark red with a purple throat) and 'Westland' (shades of rose-red).

S. truncata

Growing to 30cm (1ft) or more tall with arching branches. Stem segments are 6.5cm (2⅔in) long, by 3cm (1¼in) wide, with two to four sharp teeth along the sides, and one at each of the upper corners. Flowers are 8cm (3in) long, petals very abruptly bent back, bright rose-pink, paler inside, opening in late autumn and winter.

SCINDAPSUS

Araceae

Scindapsus pictus

Origin: *S.E. Asia from China to Malaysia. A genus of about 20 species of evergreen climbers allied to* Philodendron. *They produce aerial roots and have smooth-edged leaves, the bases of the stalks sheathing the stem. The flowers are arum-like. The species described below is a good house and conservatory plant. Propagate by cuttings, or by layering in summer.* Scindapsus *is the ancient Greek name for a climbing plant akin to ivy.*

Species cultivated

S. pictus Malaysia, Indonesia

Growing to 2m (6½ft) in pots, and climbing to 12m (40ft) or more in the wild. Leaves are 10–15cm (4–6in) long, oval to heart-shaped, dark green patterned with lighter green. *S.p.* 'Argyraeus' (*Pothos argyraeus*, Silver vine) is probably a juvenile form, having slender stems and smaller leaves with silvery spots; this is the form most commonly available as a houseplant.

SINNINGIA
Gesneriaceae

Origin: *Mexico to Argentina. A genus of about 75 species, including plants formerly classified as* Corytholoma, Gesneria, Gloxinia *and* Rechsteineria. *Most grow from somewhat woody tubers and have erect to ascending stems. Their leaves are oval and the tubular, five-lobed flowers can be solitary or borne in cymes from the upper leaf axils. Pot tubers in spring and dry off when the leaves yellow in autumn, storing in their pots at not less than 12°C (52°F) for the winter. Propagate by cuttings off those young shoots with at least two pairs of leaves, preferably with a sliver of tuber attached; these need bottom heat of 21–24°C (70–75°F) and are best in a propagating case. Tubers can be cut into sections, each with a young shoot. Dust the cut area with a fungicide and pot at once. Seed can be sown in warmth in spring.* Sinningia *was named for Wilhelm Sinning (1794–1874), a German gardener.*

Sinningia speciosa

Species cultivated

S. speciosa (*Gloxinia speciosa*) Gloxinia Brazil

The true species is 15–25cm (6–10in) tall. Leaves are 15–20cm (6–8in) long, oval to oblong, with velvety hairs, dark green above, flushed with red beneath. The red to violet flowers grow to a length of 4–5cm (1½–2in) long, are solitary, nodding, rather like a foxglove but with a fleshy texture, opening in summer. Most frequently cultivated under this name are two hybrid groups of involved parentage (sown at intervals with sufficient warmth they can be kept in bloom throughout the year): *Maxima group* (*Gloxinia × maxima*) Plants have larger, more fleshy-textured nodding flowers which range from pinks and reds to purple and white or can be bicoloured. *Fyfiana group* (*Gloxinia × fyfiana, G. × hybrida*) Similarly larger, fleshier flowers than the true species, which are more erect and bell-shaped and sometimes have waved or crimped petals; they can be either single or double and come in a similar range of colours to the Maxima group.

SMITHIANTHA

Gesneriaceae

Origin: Mexico. A genus of four species of perennials formerly named Naegelia. They have fleshy, tuber-like rhizomes and erect stems which carry pairs of broadly oval, velvety leaves and nodding, tubular, five-lobed flowers rather like foxgloves, on long stalks in summer and autumn. They make handsome pot plants. Propagate by separating the rhizomes when potting in late winter and early spring. Potting some every three to four weeks will extend the flowering season. Smithiantha was named for Matilda Smith (1854–1926), a botanical artist working at Kew.

Smithiantha 'Karen'

Species cultivated

S. cinnabarina Temple bells Mexico

Growing from 40–60cm (16–24in) tall with red-hairy leaf stalks. Leaves are 8–15cm (3–6in) long, deep green and purple with velvety red-brown hairs giving a glossy effect. Flowers reach a length of 4cm (1½in), are brick-red to scarlet and often lined with creamy-yellow.

S. zebrina Mexico

This species reaches a height of 75cm (2½ft). The dark green leaves grow to 18cm (7in) and are patterned with purplish-brown. Flowers are 4cm (1½in) long, the tube is scarlet above and golden beneath with upper lobes orange-yellow, lower yellow.

Hybrid cultivars

These two species and others have been hybridized together to produce a race of strong-growing cultivars with freely borne flowers forming pyramid-shaped panicles. They are available in a wide colour range including scarlet, carmine, pink, orange, yellow and white, with varying amounts of bronzing on the leaves.

SPATHIPHYLLUM

Araceae

Origin: *Tropical areas of Central and South America, and the islands of S.E. Asia. A genus of about 35 species of evergreen perennials with long-stalked oval to lance-shaped leaves forming dense clumps. They are good tub or pot plants for the conservatory or home needing a humid atmosphere. Propagate by division when repotting.* Spathiphyllum *derives from the Greek* spathe, *bract and* phyllon, *leaf, the spathes being leaf-like in shape.*

Spathiphyllum wallisii

Species cultivated

S. × 'Mauna Loa'

This is a hybrid with a very involved parentage. It is vigorous and compact, 45–60cm (1½–2ft) tall. The dark green leaves are oblong and lance-shaped, and reach a length of 30cm (1ft). The white spathes are 13–20cm (5–8in) long.

S. wallisii Peace lily, White sails Colombia and Venezuela

This perennial reaches a height of 30–45cm (1–1½ft). Leaves are 15–25cm (6–10in) long, oblong to lance-shaped, glossy green. The white spathes grow to 13cm (5in) or more long and are oval.

STEPHANOTIS

Asclepiadaceae

Origin: *Malagasy, southern Asia east to Malaysia and Peru. A genus of about 15 species of woody climbers with opposite, undivided, usually leathery-textured leaves and jasmine-like tubular flowers opening to five spreading lobes. The species described below is a handsome container plant, needing canes, wires or a trellis to support the long, twining shoots. Prune in winter before new growth is made. Propagate by seed or semi-hardwood cuttings in summer, both in heat, or by layering.* Stephanotis *derives from the Greek* stephanos, *crown and* otis, *ear, referring to the crown of stamens which have outgrowths supposedly like ears.*

Stephanotis floribunda

Species cultivated

S. floribunda Madagascar jasmine Malagasy

Evergreen climber which can be kept to a height of 60cm (2ft) by twining around a low support, but is capable of reaching 5m (16ft) or more. Leaves grow in opposite pairs, 5–10cm (2–4in) long, broadly elliptic with a mucronate tip, glossy dark green. Flowers are about 4cm (1½in) long, white, waxy-textured and fragrant. They are borne in axillary cymes from spring to autumn.

STREPTOCARPUS

Gesneriaceae
Cape primroses

Origin: *Tropical to southern Africa and Malagasy. A genus of 132 species of evergreen perennials, monocarps and annuals which can be grouped into three distinct growth forms. These are tufted or clump-forming with basal leaves; shrub-like with pairs of small leaves on branched stems; or unifoliate, a curious development with each plant producing one very much enlarged cotyledon and occasionally a few small basal leaves, the plant usually dies after flowering (monocarpic). The flowers are normally tubular to funnel-shaped, opening to five rounded, spreading lobes and followed by slender, pod-like capsules which are spirally twisted. The species described below are suitable for the conservatory or home, needing extra humidity in summer. Propagate the tufted sorts by leaf or leaf section cuttings, the shrubby species by stem cuttings, both in summer, and all species by seed in spring.* Streptocarpus *derives from the Greek* streptos, *twisted and* karpos, *a fruit; the slender seed pods are longitudinally spirally twisted.*

Streptocarpus × *hybrids*
'Albatross'

Streptocarpus primulifolius

Species cultivated

S. primulifolius South Africa

Tufted to clump-forming, with tongue- to strap-shaped, arching leaves, 30–45cm (1–1½ft) in length. Flowers are 6–11cm (2½–4½in) long, narrowly funnel-shaped with blue-purple lobes. One to four flowers are carried on each 25cm (10in) high stem.

S. rexii Cape primrose South Africa

Of tufted to clump-forming habit. Leaves are 10–25cm (4–10in) long, narrowly oblong, wrinkled and hairy, and edged with shallow, rounded teeth. Flowers are 4–7cm (1½–2¾in) long, funnel-shaped, mauve to blue-purple, and carried in clusters of one to six on 10–15cm (4–6in) tall stems. It is confused in cultivation with its hybrids.

Hybrids

S. × hybridus Garden origin

Under this name are grouped the varied results of crossing a dozen or so species of streptocarpus. In appearance, the plants resemble *S. rexii,* but the tufted leaves are larger, the funnel-shaped flowers also larger and variably coloured. These are mainly sold as seed mixtures under such names as Mixed Hybrids, Prize Strain, Triumph Hybrids and 'Concord'. The colour range of these mixtures covers shades of purple, blue, red, pink and white, usually with throat stripes of a contrasting colour. Individual flowers are trumpet-shaped with five broadly rounded lobes and can reach 8cm (3in) across.

STROBILANTHES

Acanthaceae

Origin: *Tropical Asia and Malagasy. A genus of about 250 species of perennials, some of which are more or less shrubby, and true shrubs. One species is grown for its highly ornamental foliage. It is best in the conservatory, but can be kept in the home at least for short periods. Propagate by cuttings in spring or summer.* Strobilanthes *derives from the Greek* strobilos, *a cone and* anthos, *a flower, referring to the bracted flower spikes of some species.*

Strobilanthes dyerianus

Species cultivated

S. dyerianus Persian shield Burma

A shrubby perennial reaching 60cm (2ft) or more in height, with erect sparingly branched stems. Leaves are in opposite pairs, narrowly oval to lance-shaped, slender-pointed and running into a winged stalk, growing to 20cm (8in) long. The upper surface of each leaf is a blend of green, purple and silver with a shimmering iridescence, and purple beneath. Flowers are 2.5–4cm (1–1½in) long, narrowly funnel-shaped with a slanting mouth and five rounded lobes, pale blue or lavender, in short, dense spikes at the ends of the stems. The slender-stemmed, willow-leaved cultivar 'Exotica' is probably a separate, un-named species.

TECOMARIA

Bignoniaceae

Origin: *Eastern and southern Africa. A genus of two or three species of shrubs and scramblers closely related to* Tecoma. *One species is widely grown in warm countries. Propagate by seed in spring or by cuttings in summer.* Tecomaria *derives from* tecoma, *indicating the close botanical relationship.*

Species cultivated

T. capensis (*Bignonia capensis, Tecoma capensis*) Cape honeysuckle South Africa

In an open site it is a bushy shrub growing to 1.2m (4ft) or more, but among other shrubs or in partial shade it produces floppy stems to

Tecomaria capensis

twice this length and becomes a semi-climber. It can be easily maintained as a bush by pinching or cutting out all extra long shoots. The dark green leaves are pinnate and composed of five to nine round to oval or diamond-shaped toothed leaflets 2.5–5cm (1–2in) long. Orange-red flowers are 5cm (2in) long, narrowly funnel-shaped, curved, with five rounded lobes which are bent back. They are borne in spring to autumn.

TREVESIA
Araliaceae

Origin: *Indo-Malaysia and Pacific. Depending upon the botanical authority, a genus of four to ten species of shrubs and small trees, some of them with wonderfully shaped leaves as though modelled on a snowflake crystal. One species is outstanding in this respect and provides a very specially decorative-foliaged pot or tub plant for the conservatory and is also worth trying in the home. Propagate by cuttings in summer or by seed in spring. Trevesia honours the family of Trèves de Bonfigli of Padua, patrons of botany in the eighteenth century.*

Trevesia palmata

Species cultivated
T. palmata Snowflake aralia N. India to S.W. China
A small tree in its homeland, but maintainable at 2m (6½ft) or less in a container. The stems are erect, sparingly branched and sometimes prickly. Leaves are alternate, long-stalked and circular in outline. They are divided into seven to 11 leaflets which are attached to the edge of a central duck's-foot-like web of leaf tissue, which radiate out from the stalk, when young the leaflets are oval with a few teeth, but when mature they become deeply cut into bluntly triangular lobes, all a deep glossy green and lightly corrugated. The leaves can vary from 25–60cm (10–24in) across, depending upon the age of the plant. Flowers are yellowish, small, in rounded umbels arranged in erect panicles, but only on mature plants.

TURNERA
Turneraceae

Origin: *Tropics and sub-tropics. A genus of about 60 species of shrubs and perennials, one of which resembles a yellow mallow and makes a showy plant for the conservatory or large room. Propagate by seed in spring or by cuttings in summer. Turnera honours William Turner (c. 1508–1568), doctor, herbalist and clergyman, now affectionately known as the 'Father of English Botany'.*

Turnera ulmifolia

Species cultivated

T. ulmifolia (*T. trioniflora*) Sage rose Mexico, West Indies, Tropical America

A shrubby plant, 60–120cm (2–4ft) tall, of somewhat spreading habit and freely branching. Leaves are oblong to oval, sharply toothed, deep green above and covered with white hairs beneath, reaching a length of 5–10cm (2–4in). Flowers are five-petalled, about 5cm (2in) wide, pale to deep yellow, and sometimes purple-tinted in bud. The flowers open soon after sunrise and close at noon, and are borne singly from the upper leaf axils in summer and autumn.

T.u. angustifolia

Lance-shaped leaves and narrower petals.

VRIESEA
Bromeliaceae

Origin: *Tropical America. A genus of 190 to 245 species, depending on the classification followed, of perennials, which are epiphytic (they grow perched on another plant in the wild). They have strap-shaped, leathery leaves in rosettes, which are often striped, netted or marbled with darker shades. The flowers are three-petalled and rather small, borne within coloured, boat-shaped bracts making up undivided or branched spikes. They can be grown either in pots or wired to a tree branch. Propagate by detaching well-rooted offsets in summer.* Vriesea *was named for the Dutch botanist Willem Hendrick de Vriese (1806–1862), professor at Leiden and Amsterdam.*

Species cultivated

V. carinata Lobster claws Brazil

Leaves grow to 20cm (8in) long, are pale green and unmarked. Flowers are 5cm (2in) long, yellow within bracts which are scarlet below and yellow above. They are borne in a broad, flattened spike on a stem up to 30cm (1ft) tall.

V. hieroglyphica King of the bromeliads Brazil

Leaves are up to 45cm (1½ft) long and 10cm (4in) wide, yellow-green above marked with brownish-green, horizontal stripes with feathered edges supposedly resembling hieroglyphics; the under surface purplish. Flowers reach a length of 3cm (1½in), are dull yellow on stems which are more than 1m (3ft) tall. A striking foliage plant.

V. splendens Flaming sword Guyana, Trinidad, Venezuela
Leaves are 40cm (16in) long, dull green, with broad horizontal brown bands. Flowers are 6cm (2½in) long, yellow, and grow within flattened scarlet bracts which make up a 45cm (1½ft) long, sword-like spike carried on a slightly shorter stem. 'Major' is brighter coloured and more robust.

Hybrids

Vriesea is perhaps the most hybridized of all the genera in the *Bromeliaceae*. The first hybrids were produced about 100 years ago and there has been a resurgence of interest during the past 40 years. On the whole, the hybrid cultivars are just as decorative as the species, in some cases more so, and they tend to be easier to grow.

V. × erecta (*V.* × *poelmannii* × *rex*) Red feather. Glossy light green foliage, deep red, waxy floral bracts and yellow flowers.

V. × 'Favourite' (*V. ensiformis* hybrid), lustrous deep green leaves, maroon floral bracts and yellow flowers.

Vriesea hieroglyphica

GLOSSARY

Alternate One leaf at each node in a staggered formation up the stem.

Anther The male part of a flower usually consisting of two lobes or 'sacs' containing pollen grains. *See* Stamen.

Areole A tiny hump-like organ found in all true members of the cactus family (*Cactaceae*), which bears bristles, spines, hairs or wool. It arises in what is technically a leaf axil, and is considered to be a highly modified shoot.

Aril An extra external coating around a seed, often fleshy and brightly coloured.

Axillary Growing from the point where a leaf or bract joins the stem.

Bipinnate Of leaves, bracts and stipules that are doubly pinnate, i.e. with leaf lobes that are again pinnate.

Bipinnatisect Of leaves, bracts or stipules that are doubly pinnatisect, i.e. with leaf lobes that are again lobed.

Bract A modified leaf usually associated with an inflorescence, in the axils of which flowers arise. Some bracts are scale-like and insignificant, others are large and coloured.

Bullate Puckered or appearing as if blistered; used of leaves where the tissue between the veins is raised up.

Bulbil Tiny bulbs or compact immature plantlets borne above ground, mainly on the stems of lilies and on the leaves of some other plants.

Calyx The whorl of sepals that protects the flower while in the bud stage.

Capsule A dry, often box-like fruit containing many seeds and opening by pores or slits, or explosively.

Channelled Used of a narrow leaf or leaflet with up-turned edges forming a channel or gutter-shape.

Cone A spike-like structure or strobilus which bears seeds (conifers) or spores (club mosses).

Corm An underground storage organ derived from a stem base.

Corolla The petals of a flower that may be separate or fused to form a funnel, trumpet or bell.

Corymb A racemose flower cluster with the stalks of the lower flowers longer than the upper ones creating a flattened or domed head.

Cultivar Short for cultivated variety and referring to a particular variant of a species or hybrid maintained in cultivation by vegetative propagation or carefully controlled seed production. Such a plant may be purposefully bred by man, or arise spontaneously as a mutation.

Cyme A compound inflorescence made up of repeated lateral branching. In the monochasial cyme each branch ends in a flower bud and one lateral branch. In the dichasial cyme each branch ends in a bud and two opposite branches.

Decumbent Having prostrate stems with the tips erect.

Digitate A compound palmate leaf (like an outspread hand) with the leaflets radiating from the top of the stalk.

Dimorphic Having two forms, e.g. some plants have two distinct types of flowers or leaves on the same plant, others have a different habit when young and adult.

Drupe A fleshy fruit, usually with one central seed.

Elliptic Usually of leaves that are broadest in the middle and taper evenly to the base and tip.

Epiphyte A plant that perches upon another, as orchids and bromeliads grow on trees. They are not parasitic, gaining moisture from rain and air, and food from humus-filled bark crevices.

Floret Tiny flowers, usually when aggregated to form larger ones as in a daisy.

Frond An alternative name for the leaf of a fern or palm.

Genus A category or classification of all living things that groups together all species with characters in common. Of the two basic scientific names which most plants have, the first is the generic, the second the species.

Glochid Tiny barbed bristle on the areole of some cacti.

Habit The general or overall appearance of a plant, e.g. erect, bushy, mat forming, etc.

Inflorescence The part of a plant that bears the flowers consisting of one or more blooms and their leafstalks and pedicels (the stalk of an individual flower). *See also* Corymb, Cyme, Panicle, Raceme, and Umbel.

Internode The length of stem between two nodes.

Keel The two lower petals of a pea flower (members of the *Leguminosae*), which are pressed together around the pistil and stamens.

Lip The colloquial name for the labellum, the lowest of the three petals in the orchid flower. It is modified in a wide variety of ways to aid pollination by insects.

Lobe A section of a leaf, bract, etc., that is partially separated from the main part of the organ like a cape or isthmus. It is used also for the petal-like divisions at the mouth of a tubular flower.

Monocarpic Of plants that flower and seed once then die. Technically, annuals and biennials are monocarpic, but horticulturally the term is used for plants that live more than two years before flowering.

Mucronate Leaves, bracts, sepals or petals that narrow abruptly at the apex, terminating in a firm, often sharp point.

Nectary A small gland, which secretes a sugary liquid (nectar). Nectaries are found mainly in flowers but sometimes elsewhere such as on leaf stalks.

Node That part of a stem where the leaf is joined and a lateral shoot grows out.

Offset Botanically, a special condensed shoot borne at the end of a short stem from the base of a plant. Horticulturally, also, used of any approximately basal shoot that can easily be detached for propagation purposes. Also used of the small, or daughter, bulbs that form beside the main one.

Opposite Of leaves or other organs borne in pairs on opposite sides of a stem.

Panicle An inflorescence of several racemes or cymes.

Pappus In general, the tuft of hairs on a seed or fruit to assist distribution by wind.

Pectinate Like the teeth of a comb; used of pinnate leaves, bracts or sepals with many narrow leaflets or lobes at right angles to the midrib. Also of leaves, bracts or petals with a fringe of coarse hairs.

Pedate A palmatisect leaf (rounded and palmately lobed almost to the base) with at least two basal lobes again lobed.

Perianth The two outer whorls (calyx and corolla or sepals and petals) that first protect and then display the generative parts. In a general way perianth is used when the petals and sepals look alike as in a tulip.

Pinnate Of a leaf composed of two ranks of leaflets on either side of the midrib.

Pinnatifid A leaf divided pinnately to half up the midrib.

Pseudobulb A swollen aerial stem typical of epiphytic orchids.

Procumbent Lying flat on the ground; in the strict sense, of stems that do not root as they grow.

Raceme An inflorescence composed of a central or main stem bearing stalked blooms at intervals.

Receptacle The usually enlarged stem tip, which bears the floral whorls (petals, sepals, etc.); also the greatly flattened stem tip which bears the florets of daisy or scabious bloom.

Rhizome A more or less underground stem that produces roots and aerial stems. In some cases they are slender and fast growing, in others fleshy with storage tissue and then elongating slowly.

Rootstock Botanically an approximately erect rhizome as found in some ferns. Horticulturally used for the ground-level junction of a compact perennial plant from which roots and leaves or stems arise. Also a horticultural term for a plant or its root system upon which another is grafted.

Scape A leafless flowering stem which arises direct from ground level, e.g. a daffodil.

Sepal The outer whorl of the perianth of a flower, usually green but sometimes coloured and then petal-like.

Spadix A thick fleshy flower spike with the small flowers embedded in pits or sitting flush with the surface; typical of arum lilies and other members of the *Araceae*.

Spathe A green or coloured petal-like bract, which surrounds or encloses the spadix, q.v.

Species A group of individual plants which breed together and have the same constant and distinctive characters, though small differences may occur.

Spore Minute reproductive bodies formed of one or a few cells together, which give rise to new individuals, either directly as in fungi, or indirectly as in ferns.

Sporangium An asexually formed spore.

Stamen The male unit of a flower comprising two anther lobes joined together at the top of a filament (stalk).

Staminode A rudimentary stamen, sometimes functioning as a petal or nectary, but usually producing no viable pollen.

Standard The upper or top petal of a pea flower, or the three inner usually upstanding petals of an iris bloom. Also a gardening term for a tree-like plant with an unbranched main stem and a head of branches.

Style The stalk that joins the pistil to the stigma.

Subshrub A small shrub that is woody at the base only, the upper part, particularly flowering stems, dying back each winter. From a gardening point of view the term is also used loosely for any low-growing softish-stemmed shrub.

Subspecies A distinct, true breeding form of a species, often isolated geographically from the species itself and differing more significantly than a variety.

Syncarp An ovary (later a seed pod or fruit) formed by the fusion of several carpels, e.g. lily, poppy, pineapple.

Tepal Used of petals and sepals combined when they look exactly alike, e.g. tulip, crocus, narcissus.

Trifoliate Mainly of leaves divided into three leaflets, but sometimes used for whorls or groups of three leaves.

Tuber Usually underground storage organs derived from stems and roots. Root tubers, e.g. dahlia, do not produce buds, new growth arising from the base of the existing or old stems. Stem tubers, e.g. potato, bear buds (the eyes of a potato) of which some form the next season's stems.

Tubercle A small wart or knob-like projection on a stem, leaf, or fruit, etc.

Umbel An inflorescence of stalked flowers all of which arise and radiate from the tip of the main stem.

Unifoliate Of plants with one leaf only. Also used of compound leaves (usually pinnate or trifoliate) that are reduced to one large leaflet only.

Variegated The white to cream or yellow markings on leaves due to lack of chlorophyll. Sometimes there are also tints of red, pink or purple. There are three primary causes: mutation, virus infection and a deficiency of an essential mineral which upsets the formation of chlorophyll.

Whorl Of leaves, bracts or flowers arranged in a ring of three or more.